Christian In Training:
A 40 Day Devotional

Pauline Creeden

An imprint of Topline Tack
Yorktown, Virginia

Copyright © 2013 Pauline Creeden
Cover Copyright © 2013 Marcy Rachel Designs

ISBN: 0615753191
ISBN-13: 978-0615753195

DEDICATION

For the horses and riders who have taught me so much.

Introduction

The relationship between horse and rider, just like nearly every other relationship, can teach us much about our relationship with God. He is our provider, our trainer, and our caregiver, much like the trainer/rider is for their horse.

Each of these devotionals are to be read in about 2 minutes. That's enough time to drink coffee and spend a moment reading and setting your day right before starting on.

Whether you love horses or only have a cursory knowledge of them, it is my hope that you'll look at scripture in a new way through this 40 day study.

Day One

He makes me lie down in green pastures, he leads me beside quiet waters. (Psalm 23:2 NIV)

Horses sleep lying down. In movies they often depict horses that lie down as sick or in pain, so most people don't know that they need to lie down to get REM sleep. If they can't lie down and get deep sleep, they become sleep deprived and develop disorders. They can have narcoleptic type fits that could cause them to fall over during times when they get a chance to relax, like while being groomed.

In order to lie down and rest, they need to be in a predictable environment with a "guard on watch." This is why you'll sometimes see one horse lying down while another stands over him. If they are in an environment that is unpredictable, they will worry about predator attacks or even attacks from other herd members that do not "like" them. If they live alone, they sometimes fear falling into deep sleep because they have no one to warn them if danger threatens.

The attribute that David ascribes to God in this Psalm is His ability to give us a place of peace and rest in our hearts. If we trust God, our hearts can become a predictable place where no worry can permeate. He will stand guard over our hearts, and will protect us from danger so we can rest.

Day Two

Is there anyone here who, planning to build a new house, doesn't first sit down and figure the cost so you'll know if you can complete it? (Luke 14:28 MSG)

One of the hardest battles a horse trainer will wage is teaching a horse to load into a trailer. When the trainer approaches the horse with a training plan in mind, she must be ready to spend as much time and energy necessary to complete the task. The trainer must not be on a time schedule or tired when she starts this work. If the trainer becomes impatient and tries to rush the horse into the trailer, the horse will become more resistant, and a bad experience might occur. Patience and energy are paramount.

When you decide to spend time with God in prayer and studying His word, patience and energy are paramount here as well. If you are tired or on a time schedule, you will be easily distracted from the important work you are doing will suffer. You cannot be looking at the clock while studying the Bible, and you don't want to spend the time constantly thinking about how you need to spend the rest of your day.

To tackle this task, consider studying and praying at a time of day when you are least likely to be distracted. Make sure that it is also a time when you have the energy to devote to God. Then give God all your attention. You will not regret making time for Him in this way!

Day Three

You shall teach them diligently to your children, and shall talk of them when you sit in your house, when you walk by the way, when you lie down, and when you rise up. (Deuteronomy 6:7 NKJV)

Because of his anatomy, the horse's stomach is constantly producing acid. He must eat all day long in order to keep from developing ulcers and other digestive issues. This is why it is suggested to split a horse's daily food intake into several small portions rather than one large one.

God has designed us spiritually in a similar manner. We need to take in nourishment from Him several times per day in order to keep the "acid" in our lives from making us upset. Reading the word, spending time in prayer, praising His name, and listening to Godly teachings are ways to get that nourishment.

Spending twenty minutes of devotional time in the morning is wonderful, but if that's all the nourishment we get, then by evening the "acid" of worry and stress in our lives will upset our witness, our progress, and our walk. We have to keep ruminating on the word all day long in order to keep our spiritual digestive system on track so that we can grow.

Day Four

To the weak I became weak, to win the weak. I have become all things to all people so that by all possible means I might save some. (1 Corinthians 9:22 NIV)

A good trainer can ride any kind of horse. She can ride with an 'aggressive leg' when the horse is lazy. She can have a gentle hand for the horse that is sensitive. She can sit like a sack of potatoes on a horse that is nervous. She has the energy to endure the fresh horse. She can instill confidence in the horse that is unsure.

As followers of Jesus, we are to become all things to all people. The good trainer above didn't change who she was, just *how she rode*. We are not supposed to change who we are. A horse can tell who is honest and who is lying just as easily as a person you're trying to witness to.

Be who you are. But when your friend is hurting – don't pretend you know the answers. Instead listen and remember that you have hurt before too. When your friend is broken, remember that you've been broken before. When your friend is sad, be a shoulder for her to cry on. When your friend is in trouble, be a help to him. Whatever your friend needs, help them.

Day Five

Anxiety weighs down the heart, but a kind word cheers it up. (Proverbs 12:25 NIV)

The symptoms of anxiety in a ridden horse include: ear-pinning, chomping at the bit, tail-wringing, and high-headedness. If the rider does not relieve his tension, the horse will begin to sweat profusely. The horse will also become prone to bucking, rearing, or bolting away. Some riders remember to use the aids of hand and leg, but often forget one of the most necessary cues – voice. A gently spoken, "Good Boy," and the reward of loosened reins can be all the horse needs to overcome his anxiety.

The symptoms of anxiety in a human include: forehead wrinkles, tense shoulders, nervous movements, and anger. If the person does not have her tension relieved, she will begin to get snappy. The anxious person will also become prone to indigestion, heart palpitations and depression. As this person's friend, it would be helpful to remind them of the good side of things and the silver lining around every cloud. Maybe this person needs a compliment or a reminder of how you are there to help him. A gently spoken word could be all that your friend needs to overcome her anxiety.

Day Six

"Be still, and know that I am God…" (Psalm 46:10 NKJV)

If the horse has no confidence in his handler, he will have a hard time standing still. While tacked up for a ride, groomed, or bathed he will fidget and dance around because he cannot calm his nerves. When a horse has confidence in his handler, he can stand still through almost anything. He will relax and let his muscles rest. His confidence can be seen in his ability to stand still and trust his handler has things under control.

When a Christian spends time worrying and fidgeting, trying to make sure that everything is going to be okay instead of trusting God to make sure things will be okay, she is like the horse with no confidence in his handler. When we trust God, we show our confidence in Him by our ability to be still. We are still when we stop worrying and wait patiently for God to give us what we need. It is through trust in His perfect control that we are able to stand perfectly still no matter what is going on inside us. We can relax and rest in our trust in Him.

Day Seven

Just say 'yes' and 'no.' When you manipulate words to get your own way, you go wrong. (Matthew 5:37 MSG)

New owners and trainers do not understand the number one law of horses: the minute your horse makes contact with you, the training session has begun. If you are feeling permissive that day, and let your horse get away with something you normally would have said "no" to – you have now trained your horse to try that bad behavior again. After all, he got away with it before, right?

The trainer needs to always have his boundaries up. If the horse is not allowed to do something, draw a boundary. If the horse is allowed push past the boundary sometimes, then he will continue to try to push the limits of what he is allowed to do. If the boundary never changes, the horse will respect it.

In life, the people around you will also test your boundaries. Whether it's your teenager who wants to push past curfew, or the coworker who tells a dirty joke – they will all test you to see what your limits are. If you are a pushover who compromises your boundaries, no one will respect you. Although it seems at first that the teen or co-worker "hates" your stringency, they will honestly respect you for it later.

Day Eight

Do not be like the horse or like the mule, which have no understanding, which must be harnessed with bit and bridle, else they will not come near you. (Psalm 32:9 NKJV)

A horse without understanding is a horse that has no relationship with his trainer. He cannot be trusted to follow you without a halter and lead rope. He cannot be ridden without a bridle and bit.

But if a strong bond and relationship is established between horse and rider, then a halter is just there for convenience, and even a bridle can become unnecessary. What keeps this horse obedient is his trust and relationship with his handler. He doesn't need to be forced to go where the handler goes. He follows because he has confidence in his handler.

This is why it's important to have the right relationship with God. He doesn't want to force us to behave and go the way he suggests. He doesn't want to put us in a bit and bridle. He doesn't want us to follow him begrudgingly because we have to. If our relationship with God is in the right place, then we will want to stay in close fellowship with Him, walking with Him, gladly going where He leads us. He is our confidence and we can completely rely on Him.

Day Nine

Brothers and sisters, I do not consider myself yet to have taken hold of it. But one thing I do: Forgetting what is behind and straining toward what is ahead, I press on toward the goal to win the prize for which God has called me heavenward in Christ Jesus. (Philippians 3:13-14 NIV)

One thing about the world of horsemanship is that you never stop learning. There is no point at which you "arrive" with nothing left to learn. Nor is there a point at which your horse can stop being trained because he is trained enough. A horse whose training has stopped will slowly deteriorate and go back to being untrained. And if you bring the horse back into training after a long hiatus, he often will be resentful and resistant to doing things he used to know very well.

Our walk with God is very much the same. If we think we have "arrived" spiritually and stop walking with God in prayer and stop studying His word, then we will deteriorate and become like the rest of the world. When we come back from this "backslidden" position, it's often harder to recover the situation that we once had. If Paul in this letter can say that he's still working and still pressing forward, think about how much farther we need to go before we will have "arrived."

PAULINE CREEDEN

Day Ten

For precept must be upon precept, precept upon precept, line upon line, line upon line; here a little, and there a little: (Isaiah 28:10 KJV)

Constant repetition is necessary when training a horse. You have to introduce the new subject to him several times, without pain, in order for him to accept the new concept. Once it's learned, the rider can let the interval between repetitions extended and not drill the horse every day. Even after it is "learned" the repetition must continue on occasion for the horse to keep the concept in their database of learned responses, or it will be dumped like junk mail.

God knows that people are this way, too. When we learn a new truth about Jesus from God's word, we have to repeat it to ourselves over and over again so that it will become ingrained in our thoughts. That's why the Bible tells us to meditate on God's word morning and night. If we let the truth slip through our grasp, it cannot help us later when temptation comes.

Jesus used Scriptures to defeat the devil when tempted in the wilderness. He showed us this so that we could learn how to respond in the trials of life. If we have God's word in our database of learned responses, it will come to our mind when temptation arrives.

Day Eleven

The Lord of hosts—regard Him as holy and honor His holy name {by regarding Him as your only hope of safety}, and let Him be your fear and let Him be your dread {lest you offend Him by your fear of man and your distrust of Him}. (Isaiah 8:13 AMP)

One of the funniest things about the horse is that he rarely knows how big he is. He tends to believe that he is about the size of his head, forgetting the rest of his body. This is why he can find simple objects like plastic bags or small dogs to be frightening.

When he trusts in his handler, the horse will stop fearing the little things. He regards his handler as his only hope of safety and, at first, will cling to him when danger appears. As his trust in his handler grows, he will start to ignore the small stuff.

Don't sweat the small stuff. If you trust God, then you will not worry about what men think of you. You will only think of God and trust Him to take care of your every need. He will defend you if you are defamed. He will take care of your reputation. There is nothing that man can do to you that God cannot take care of. You just need to regard Him as your only hope of safety.

Day Twelve

The LORD Almighty is the one you are to regard as holy, He is the one you are to fear, He is the one you are to dread. (Isaiah 8:13 NIV)

Even though the horse was one of the first domesticated animals, he still lives in fear. The most sensitive of a horse's instincts is their 'fight or flight' instinct. This instinct causes some horses to be considered brave and others to be called 'chickens'.

The amazing part is that even the 'chickens' can become brave when they trust and respect their trainer. If they are more afraid of disappointing the trainer and getting reprimanded, they will ignore the object of their fear. When they are alone with the object, they will often revert to flight. But in the presence of their trusted trainer, they show no fear whatsoever.

This is the kind of 'fear' that the Lord demands. If we don't fear God, than we will be afraid of everything else. If we don't trust His guidance and fear His disappointment, then we will run away from everything that threatens us.

We are more fortunate than the horse, however, because we will never be alone with the object of our fear. We never need to revert to flight. Our trainer is always present. We only need to trust Him, and our fear will subside.

Day Thirteen

And do not be conformed to this world, but be transformed by the renewing of your mind, that you may prove what is that good and acceptable and perfect will of God. (Romans 12:2 NKJV)

As a horse becomes better trained, he starts to accept the aids and commands of his trainer rather than reacting to external stimuli. At first, the trainer only makes small demands of the horse: turning at the appropriate times, stopping when asked, going when prompted. As the horse listens to these easier commands, the trainer will ask for more precise movements. Because the horse becomes focused on what the trainer asks of him, the things that demanded attention before get no consideration at all. Other horses, strange noises and sights no longer gain his interest.

If our focus on God becomes fine tuned by the renewing of our mind, we will become more precise in the action of performing His will in our lives. The outside clamor of people to see, places to go, things to do will fall into the background and draw less and less of our interest. We will find that we are not molded by the environment we are in, but rather the training that God has placed within us.

Day Fourteen

My grace is sufficient for you, for my power is made perfect in weakness. Therefore I will boast all the more gladly about my weakness, so that Christ's power may rest on me. (2 Corinthians 12:9 NIV)

A horse that is out of work is out of shape. His muscles are flabby, and after working for about fifteen minutes, he's out of breath and breaking a sweat. He is weak, flabby, and the only power found in him is potential. Like a horse in the wild, he is only good as a meal for a lion. A good trainer brings the potential out of the horse and turns it into power. With the trainer's help, the horse gains stamina, muscle, and fitness.

When we first come to Christ, our spiritual muscles are flabby, and we have no endurance when resisting temptation. We are weak, and all our power is in our potential. It takes God to bring out our potential. We cannot do it ourselves. Without Him, we will be weak and flabby – giving in to every temptation and finding ourselves the meal of Satan. But with God's guidance, we can gain strength, stamina and spiritual fitness.

Day Fifteen

A man's heart plans his way, but the Lord directs his steps. (Proverbs 16:9 NIV)

A trainer may enter the work arena with a specific plan for what she wants to get done. But if the wind is up or the horse has an attitude – the trainer needs to be ready to change plans. Depending on what is necessary for achieving a good training session, she needs to go in with a plan but be flexible. Inflexibility makes for a frustrated horse or trainer.

How many times have you made a plan for your day and end up having your plans ruined by the weather or other people? Do you bend and flex, adapt and make sure that the day is still a good one? Or do you stay stiff-necked and allow your day to be ruined because it didn't go according to plan?

Next time things don't go according to plan, think about being flexible and see what kind of day God has planned for you. If you keep in mind that God will direct your steps in the direction He wants you to go today, you may not become so easily frustrated when things take a turn. Trust Him to know better than you.

Day Sixteen

Those who live as their human nature tells them to, have their minds controlled by what human nature wants. Those who live as the Spirit tells them to, have their minds controlled by what the Spirit wants. (Romans 8:5 NIV)

Wild horses have the appearance of freedom, but they are enslaved by their fear. They have to be on constant alert for the danger of predators. They can only hope to find shelter when inclement weather strikes. They fear being alone, but the herd could reject them. Their lack of grooming gives them skin infections, and ticks eat them alive in the summer. When winter comes and the grass becomes sparse or in times of drought, they could easily die. They are rarely calm or content.

When a horse is being tamed, they certainly don't look happy. They buck and rear. They run from their handler. They "spook" and shy away from anything that looks dangerous. They fear the change that taming brings, and they fear their handler.

But the tame horse is the happy one. He does not fear when his next meal will come. He learns to trust that his handler will keep him safe from predators. Daily grooming keeps infections and ticks at bay. When inclement weather strikes, he has a roof over his head. He has no fear, because he has learned trust.

Have we learned to trust our God? Or do we demand our freedom from Him and live in fear?

Day Seventeen

Ponder the path of your feet, and let all your ways be established. Do not turn to the right or to the left; remove your foot from evil. (Proverbs 4:27-28 NKJV)

Horses do not naturally go in straight lines. They tend to weave to the left and right as they move, like any wild prey animal. Even when they follow a well worn path created by other wild animals, you should notice that the path is rarely straight. This is a survival characteristic among prey animals.

When a rider first begins to train a horse, she has to teach the horse to go straight. With gentle nudges from her leg and hand, the horse slowly begins to learn his boundaries. Some horses need a great deal of coaxing to learn straightness. Some will even require spurs to become more sensitive.

A well trained horse is a straight horse.

Humans are much the same way. We wander and become easily distracted, rarely going in a straight line. But if we listen to God's gentle nudges, we too can learn to go straight. God, like a rider, may have to use increasingly hard "nudges" to get our attention. But He is a kind trainer who wants us to become sensitive to the smallest cue. I pray that we remain sensitive to His gentleness, so He will not need to bring out His spurs.

Day Eighteen

A gentle answer turns away wrath, but a harsh word stirs up anger. (Proverbs 15:1 NIV)

Horses need praise. If the rider is the type that only punishes bad behavior while never giving the horse a pat and a "good boy," the horse will respond in one of two ways. The eager to please horse will become a nervous wreck: chewing the bit, tilting the head, and constantly looking for the reward so he can relax. The more willful horse will become angry and frustrated, he will give up on trying to be good and start a fight instead.

Humans need praise. This is the reason that the 'Law' was superseded by 'Grace'. The law gave stringent rules along with punishments, but rarely gave rewards. Grace is a reward all in itself.

People, like horses, will respond to the unbending law in the same two ways. Those who try hard to please a God that seems "un-please-able" will become neurotic and develop superstitions. The person who is more headstrong will become angry and frustrated, give up trying, and quit the whole "religious thing" altogether.

We need to remember that God gives us salvation as a free gift. No good behavior on our part will ever earn it. The praise is there for the taking.

Day Nineteen

Walk with me and work with me – watch how I do it. Learn the unforced rhythms of grace. I won't lay anything heavy or ill-fitting on you. (Matthew 11:29 MSG)

The saddle and equipment that a rider puts on the horse must fit appropriately. If the saddle is too narrow, it will pinch the horse's back muscles causing soreness and stiffness. If the saddle is too wide, it will rub on the horse's withers and cause an open, bleeding sore. If the bridle is adjusted too loosely, the horse's tongue will go over the bit causing pain when the rider uses the reins. If the bridle is adjusted too tightly, it will pinch the horse's face and mouth.

Jesus has promised that He will not lay anything heavy or ill-fitting on you. If you are finding your walk with Him too cumbersome, then you may be trying to do too much on your own. Remember that GRACE is a gift, and there is nothing you can do to earn it. It's hard when you've grown up being independent, and not looking for a hand-out, to accept God's gift without earning it. But remember that the burden of our sin and the worries of this life are too much for us to carry on our own.

Day Twenty

They are like children sitting in the marketplace and calling to one another, saying: "We played the flute for you, and you did not dance; we mourned to you, and you did not weep." (Luke 7:32 NKJV)

When the horse believes that he knows what the rider wants, he will try to give it to her before she asks, believing that he is being obedient. When the rider corrects the horse and tries to teach him to be patient, often he will become indignant. He will be offended by her attempts to correct him because he believes that he knows better.

This becomes a difficult training point for the rider who has to reteach the horse to be obedient, and implement new training methods to 'surprise' the horse. The horse must learn that he is not the one who controls the ride, nor can he be the one who decides where the rider wants to go or how fast they will get there.

God will not usually behave the way that we expect Him to. He will not do what we want Him to do, when we want Him to do it. We do not decide where we go, or how fast we get there. Instead of becoming offended by His leading, we need to trust it and be patient. We cannot anticipate Him, nor can we put Him in a box and think He should behave a certain way. He will always surprise us.

Day Twenty-One

The one who searches for what is good finds favor, but if someone looks for trouble, it will come to them. (Proverbs 11:27 NIV)

When a handler goes into a training session with a horse, her attitude can have a huge impact on the outcome of the session. If the handler has a good attitude, then the horse will feed off that attitude and respond with more willingness to give in. If the handler is itching for a fight, then a fight she shall receive.

Our attitudes cause us to have either a good day or a bad one. If we go into our day looking for the silver lining to every cloud, we'll see them. But if we go into our day looking for a fight, we'll likely find one. If we believe that God honestly does everything for our good, then we will trust Him when the storm comes. But if we don't trust Him with our lives, then we will find fear encroaching, and fear always brings resentment. Only by trusting God can we keep fear and resentment from our lives.

Day Twenty-Two

Jabez called on the God of Israel saying, "Oh that You would bless me indeed, and enlarge my territory, that Your hand would be with me, and that You would keep me from evil, that I may not cause pain!" So God granted him what he requested. (1 Chronicles 4:10 NKJV)

When training a young horse, the trainer always begins in a small area. It can be a round pen, on a lunge line, or even the corner of a larger arena. Regardless, the area where the horse begins its training is small. As the horse shows obedience, the trainer will enlarge the borders of the territory the horse is allowed to roam. Trust is first established in a small space, then a large arena, and eventually open fields and trails.

Can God trust you enough to enlarge your borders? God is one that always trusts us with the small stuff before expanding our territory. Between the Road to Damascus and when Paul started to preach, God trusted him with small stuff for nearly twenty years. Once Paul proved himself trustworthy with the big stuff, God gave him Rome.

If you find yourself longing to roam the open fields and trails, first establish yourself within the small arena where God has put you.

Day Twenty-Three

**So he answered and said to his father, "Lo, these
many years I have been serving you; I never
transgressed your commandment at any time;
and yet you never gave me a young goat, that I
might make merry with my friends. But as soon
as this son of yours came, who has devoured
your livelihood with harlots, you killed the fatted
calf for him." (Luke 15:29-30 NKJV)**

Rider 1 watches Rider 2 have a perfect round in the
horse show arena. Rider 1 thinks to herself, "I bet
that rider spent a lot of money on that horse,
because the horse is a natural. The trainer probably
rides the horse more than Rider 2 does!"

Rider 2 thinks: "Wow, all that hard work is finally
paying off! This horse that everyone else gave up
on has finally come around and performs for me.
It's amazing that he didn't buck me off today."

Before making a judgment call on how easy
someone else's life has been, we need to remember
that we all have it rough. We live in a fallen world.
That means NO ONE has a perfect life. No one who
is happy with where they are will remain that way
for very long. This Earth is not our home. The older
brother in the story of the Prodigal had no idea what
his younger brother had gone through. He envied

his brother's freedom and reward, without ever knowing what it was like to starve in a pig pen.

Day Twenty-Four

For My thoughts are not your thoughts nor are your ways My ways," says the Lord. "For as the heavens are higher than the earth, so are My ways higher than your ways, and My thoughts than your thoughts. (Isaiah 55:8-9 NIV)

When a horse becomes tame and experienced, he begins to think that he knows what the rider is going to want from him. He starts to try to predict when the rider will ask for a faster gait, and jumps ahead. He tries to predict when the rider will want to slow down, and breaks gait before the rider is ready.

The horse has crossed the fine line between being obedient and being impatient.

Often in our walk with God we believe we are being obedient, but we are truly being impatient. There are times when we believe we've heard from God and we jump ahead into doing what we think He wants. Usually this is without really talking to Him about it, and then we ask Him to bless it.

Will God bless this kind of behavior? It's when we think that we are wise that we start to make fools of ourselves. When we are prompted by the Spirit we need to pray until we know that it's God's will, instead of just guessing. We need to remember that

we are guided by Him always, and never try to take
the bit and get ahead of Him.

Day Twenty-Five

Oh, fear the Lord, you His saints! There is no want to those who fear Him. (Psalm 34:9 NKJV)

The average lifespan of the wild horse is ten years. The average domesticated horse's lifespan is 20-30 years. That's almost triple the lifespan of the wild one.

The upkeep of the horse requires twice yearly vaccinations, because they are susceptible to many communicable diseases. They must be dewormed every 6-8 weeks because they are prone to parasites. Their teeth must be ground down at least once every year to keep sharp points from developing that will cause mouth sores. They must eat almost 2% of their body weight every day in order to stay at a healthy weight.

As high maintenance as the horse is, humans require so much more upkeep! We need food, clothing, and shelter, to be sure. But inside us there is also this empty place, a hunger and a thirst that cannot be filled with just anything we want to put there.

Pascal describes a "God-shaped" vacuum within our hearts. We often try to fill it with our own addictions: sports, food, alcohol, control of our children, or even our husbands. But in none of these things will we find ourselves FULFILLED.

Because God can fill that vacuum in our hearts, we can be filled. He promises that we will not be in want if we trust, respect, and fear Him. He will take care of us and fulfill our every need.

Day Twenty-Six

"Come to me, all of you who are tired from carrying heavy loads, and I will give you rest. Take my yoke and put it on you, and learn from me, because I am gentle and humble in spirit; and you will find rest. For the yoke I will give you is easy, and the load I will put on you is light." (Matthew 11: 28-30 GNTD)

A rider's actual weight has little to do with whether they feel heavy or light to the horse. A heavy rider who has learned to stay still and is gentle to the horse is preferred over a small rider who moves around too much, pounds the horse's back with their weight and yanks the horse's mouth with their hands. The horse would choose the educated rider who works with his motion over the novice rider who works against him.

Jesus is the most educated of handlers. He will always guide us in a gentle and quiet way. No matter what we are going through, if He is our leader, we do not need to worry about the pain He will cause us in addition to the trial we are going through. Instead, Jesus works with us, lightening our load, and making it possible to do the impossible as long as He is our partner.

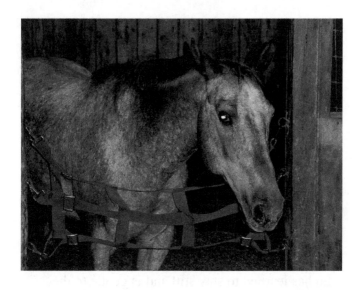

Day Twenty-Seven

This is what the Lord says: "Stand at the crossroads and look; ask for the ancient paths, ask where the good way is, and walk in it, and you will find rest for your souls."(Jeremiah 6:16 NIV)

New equipment, teaching methods, videos and tricks to train horses appear on the shelves of tack shops all the time. Every year, a new and fashionable training method becomes the "in" thing to getting a better performance out of the horse. There are clinicians who sell videos and books like hotcakes because training horses is an art form that everyone thinks that they can learn by teaching themselves. So-called trainers are a "dime a dozen" and it's difficult to find a trainer that is the right fit for the owner and horse's needs.

Likewise, there are always new tricks, videos, and teaching methods that try to put a new "spin" on Christianity. New and fashionable preachers and pastors sell videos, books, and host conferences trying to teach you a new method for talking to God or getting what you want from Him. These sell like hotcakes because people are always looking to learn about God without reading the Bible or learning from the Holy Spirit, Himself. It is difficult to go along the ancient paths that have worked for thousands of years so that we find rest and peace.

Day Twenty-Eight

There was a man of the Pharisee sect, Nicodemus, a prominent leader among the Jews. Late one night he visited Jesus and said, "Rabbi, we all know you're a teacher straight from God. No one could do all the God-pointing, God-revealing acts you do if God weren't in on it." (John 3:1-2 MSG)

There are horses that cling to their owners with great affection – when there are no other horses around. They are the ones that run to the gate when the owner calls, as long as they're turned out alone. If they are in the herd, well, the owner can call all she wants – this horse is too busy for her.

God doesn't want us to praise Him only at night, when no one can see us, judge us, or call us Jesus Freaks. He doesn't want us to be willing to answer His call only when it's convenient, or when we're ready to. He wants us to come every time He calls. Whether we are alone, at work, in a crowd of unbelievers, or at dinner with our family, He wants to be first priority.

Nicodemus came in the middle of the night when no one was around, because he was afraid of what people would think if he came in broad daylight. God wants us to talk to Him and about Him without fear of what someone else might think. He wants us in the night and in the day. He wants us in the crowd and when we're alone.

Day Twenty-Nine

So let's not allow ourselves to get fatigued doing good. At the right time we will harvest a good crop if we don't give up or quit. (Galatians 6:9 MSG)

There are times when a rider wants to give up on what she believes she should be working on in order to go for the "short cut." This is especially true when it comes to putting the horse in the proper frame. The rider knows that she is supposed to drive the horse forward into the bit with a soft hand, and that eventually the horse's head will come down and his jaw will become soft. But it takes patience and consistency. The last thing that the rider needs to do is dump all her hard work and run for the short cut. The short cut will never get you the same results that patience would have rewarded.

For the follower of God, the same is true. We should not give up on doing good when we can't see the results. If no one is grateful for your kindness, if no one notices the good you've done, and if it seems the whole world is even against what you are doing: Don't give up. Keep praying, keep trusting God. Do not go for the short cut when it comes. Be patient, your reward is just around the bend.

Day Thirty

A wise, mature person is known for his understanding. The more pleasant his words, the more persuasive he is. (Proverbs 16:21 GNTD)

The mature horse trainer has already learned this truth. When she comes up to a new horse, she understands that she needs to develop a relationship with him. Trust can only be earned by persuasive words, patience, and gentle hands. She is not looking for a fight, but building a foundation that will allow her to develop a willing partner in the horse.

God wants a relationship with you. If you are studying the Bible, you will develop the understanding that it is God's love letter to you. "God so loved YOU that He gave His only begotten son, that if YOU would believe in Him, YOU would not perish but have everlasting life." He doesn't want a slave. He wants a relationship. He wants a willing partner.

His pleasant words will persuade you to love Him if you will let them.

Day Thirty-One

She does her work with vigor and is able to get things done because her body is prepared for the tasks. (Proverbs 31:17 NIV)

Without proper training and a proper warm-up the horse cannot possibly be ready for upper level tasks. If the horse lacks proper training, frustration at the rider's aids will occur. Fear will become a problem, as the horse will not know what to expect. The horse will live under general duress and stress. If the horse lacks a proper warm-up, even if it has the training, it could be injured by the task.

As Christians, we have upper level tasks that can be expected of us. If we don't have the proper training, we will rely on our own strength to perform the tasks and we will easily become frustrated, stressed, and afraid of God asking us to do something we're not ready for. If we don't warm up through prayer and studying the Bible, even if we have the proper "training," we'll still try to do things ourselves and end up injuring our faith or someone else's. It is important to be up to the task we undertake.

Day Thirty-Two

"But what do you think? A man had two sons.
He went to the first and said, 'My son, go, work
in the vineyard today.'

He answered, 'I don't want to!' Yet later he
changed his mind and went.

Then the man went to the other son and said the
same thing.

'I will, sir,' he answered. But he didn't go.
(Matthew 21:28-30 GNTD)

There are two ways that a horse avoids going in the
direction he is steered. Usually the horse is prone to
choosing one method, not both. In the first method,
a horse will stiffen his jaw and neck and refuse to
turn his head in that direction. In the other method,
the horse will turn his head readily, but drop his
shoulder in the opposite direction and continue in
the direction he wants to go.

Both are like the parable of these sons.

The stiff horse can easily be coaxed into the new
direction by the rider using a series of 'pressure and
release' of the rein. As the stiff horse learns to
respond to the riders cues he will soften his jaw
over time and do as the rider commands. The
rubbernecking horse is much more difficult, as he

must be ridden with a great deal of leg. He can never be cured of the problem, and will always revert to rubbernecking when asked to go a direction he doesn't want to go.

Jesus prefers the stiff jaw to the rubber neck. He doesn't want your words. He wants your actions. What is He asking you to do today? If you've told Him you will – follow through!

Day Thirty-Three

A righteous man regards the life of his animal, but the tender mercies of the wicked are cruel. (Proverbs 12:10 GNTD)

There are some owners and trainers who genuinely care about the well-being of their animal. They remember that the horse is prone to having good days and bad. The horse gets tired and can also feel bored. A good trainer will always vary her training sessions so that the horse doesn't experience fatigue or boredom. This trainer is also ready to change the course of her training plans if the horse is having one of those "off" days.

On the other hand, there are owners who think of their animals as robots or disposable and temporary. They intend to get every good use out of their horse before tossing them aside and getting the next one. Even when they give the horse a "treat" it is in a selfish and cruel way. For example, fat horses look better in the horseshow arena, but are prone to many diseases such as laminitis and colic.

God is merciful. He values mercy and love above all other virtues. We should strive to be the kind of friend to others as He is to us and be forgiving of one another's bad days. We should be ready to change our plans if our friend needs us to move in a different direction. If we worry only about our inconvenience, we are being selfish.

Day Thirty-Four

I pray, let me cross over and see the good land beyond the Jordan, those pleasant mountains, and Lebanon. But the Lord was angry with me on your account and would not listen to me. So the Lord said to me: 'Enough of that! Speak no more to Me of this matter.' (Deuteronomy 3:24-25 NKJV)

There are some horses that seem to be "born broke." This means that they take little to no effort to train to become rideable. Then there is the horse that bucks, shies, rears, resists steering, resists the rider's leg, and refuses to carry a rider's weight willingly. Eventually, through a patient and consistent trainer who is sensitive to the horse's needs, the "rogue" will come around.

Unfortunately, a lot of damage can be done to the rogue before it is gentled. The act of bucking and shying puts unnecessary strain on his back and joints. His mouth may become sore from his resistance, and he could end up with lasting scars. This is not because the rider ever punished the horse, but because the horse's actions caused pain and injury.

Our sin is often this way. When we choose to sin there are consequences. If you are under Christ, you may not be punished FOR your sin anymore, but you might still be punished BY your sin. Sin leaves scars, and sometimes they never heal.

Day Thirty-Five

"You will not need to fight in this battle. Position yourselves, stand still and see the salvation of the Lord, who is with you, O Judah and Jerusalem! Do not fear or be dismayed; tomorrow you go out against them for the Lord is with you." (2 Chronicles 20:17)

In the wild, a horse that stands still for long will likely become dinner for a predator. Naturally, the horse fidgets constantly and is in constant motion. Unless he is asleep with others around him standing guard, the horse's movement is incessant. Like a coiled spring they are always ready to bounce into motion and run away from danger.

The tame horse has to learn to stand still with a rider on him. The trained rider knows she can only ask the horse to stand still for short periods at first. In the first session, the horse might only stand still for a couple of seconds, but it can slowly be extended to several minutes. The horse will trust the rider to be the watchman and relax under the rider's control, even standing still.

The battle is the Lord's. He doesn't ask us to do much more than pray, have faith, and stand still to wait for Him. As we learn to wait, He will start with short periods. Eventually the wait time is extended so that we can learn patience and trust in or God.

This is a sign that our own relationship with God is becoming stronger as we grow in our faith.

Day Thirty-Six

Oh taste and see that the Lord is good; Blessed is the man who trusts in Him. (Psalm 34:8 NKJV)

Horses, like humans, have sensitive stomachs. But what makes a horse's stomach even more sensitive is that they have a one way valve in their esophagus. This means that food goes down but nothing, not even gas, comes back up through the horse's mouth. So whatever goes into the horse has to go all the way through the horse before it can come out. Whatever bad thing that is eaten will do all its damage before leaving the system.

Spiritually, we are a lot like the horse. Whatever we take in, good or bad, tends to stay inside us. The good things bring us closer to God, while the bad drive us further away. Remember the song from Sunday school "Be careful little eyes what you see?" We have to be careful what we take in!

In this Scripture, God wants us to know that we can take Him in, and trust that He is always good for us. Even better is that when we take Him in, He heals us from all the bad stuff we consumed in the past. He heals us from the damage of our past. He is only waiting for us to taste and see.

Day Thirty-Seven

And in that day I will set apart the land of Goshen, in which my people dwell, that no swarms of flies shall be there, in order that you may know that I am the Lord in the midst of the land. (Exodus 8:22 NIV)

Flying vectors are of a particular annoyance to horses. Barn/stable flies look exactly like the common housefly, but with one major difference: they bite. Any exposed skin below the horse's or handler's knees is fair game for their blood sucking ways. Additionally, mosquitoes, giant horseflies, no-see-ums and gnats plague the horse in an attempt to suck their blood.

Imagine the constant annoyance of flies. Don't you often feel annoyed this way by worry? It is a constant distraction. If you look at this allegory, you'll see why Jesus constantly spoke to His children, telling them not to worry. If we cast our cares on Him, we should see that the swarm of worry will not alight upon God's people. The lack of worry should show the difference between those who know Him and those who do not know.

This is one of the ways that we are to be different from the rest of the world. Just like horses, people are plagued with swarms of worry. But our trust in Jesus, laying the worries at His feet, will cause the swarms to leave us alone. They will not bother us. It will be a witness to the rest of the world, and they will want to learn how to have what we have.

Day Thirty-Eight

Jesus answered, "I am telling you the truth: you are looking for me because you ate the bread and had all you wanted, not because you understood my miracles." (John 6:26 GNTD)

There are some horses that will stand in the pasture and refuse to come if you go there empty-handed. Some will run away and stay just out of your reach unless you have food for them. The handler can spend hours working with this horse, but the horse just won't come without the bribe of a treat. In opposition, there are other horses who genuinely love spending time with the owner and come to her call whether she has a treat or not.

The people in the passage of Scripture above behaved this way. They followed after Jesus because He fed them and wanted what He could do for them. They didn't understand their need for a relationship with the one behind the miracles.

What do we expect from God? Do we only look to Him for comfort? Are our only prayer times when we are not doing well and want Him to make things better? Or do we come to Him in prayer and praise whether we feel like it or not?

If He has asked us to do something, do we worry about whether He will take care of our needs first?

Do we trust Him to take care of our every need? Or do we worry that He'll forget about them? I hope we think about our expectations of God and realize that the small treats of comfort, security, and prosperity are temporary in comparison to our relationship with Jesus.

Day Thirty-Nine

Better a dry crust with peace than a house full of feasting with strife. (Proverbs 17:1 GNTD)

Horses live this proverb. Horses do not do well in strange or unpredictable environments while eating. If there is too much strife or worry in the horse's life, he will either be unable to eat at all or will develop ulcers. If the stress is extreme or the horse sensitive, he can even colic (develop a strong stomach ache) or die if the stress is not relieved.

People have the same possible outcome, but it usually doesn't come on as fast. We can go about for years in a stressful situation and live on digestive antacids instead of facing up to it. Science has even proven that a stressed person's lifespan is shortened considerably over those who have peace in their lives. Stress leads to high blood pressure, heart palpitations, and has even been linked to cancer.

God does not want us to live a life of stress. He wants us to have peace by trusting Him and letting Him care for us. If we give our cares to God, it is not the same as giving up. In some ways it is the opposite of giving up because we have to willfully stop ourselves from taking the cares back and worrying on them more. Only by giving our cares to Him, sometimes over and over again, can we gain the peace we need. And just like with any sort of newly learned behavior it will take time to learn to leave your cares where they belong.

Day Forty

For the vision is yet for the appointed time; it testifies about the end and will not lie. Though it delays, wait for it, since it will certainly come and not be late (Habakkuk 2:3 GNTD)

Horses are creatures of habit. Within them is an internal clock that reminds them of the time of day. If the horse comes in from the pasture for feeding at 4 pm, at 4 pm he will be waiting at the gate for his owner. This is a huge convenience for the owner who won't need to call him in or go out to the field to catch him.

So what happens when the owner runs late? Some horses will patiently wait at the gate. Others will demand to come in by pawing or pacing at the gate. They will wait for a very long time before giving up and heading back into the pasture if the owner tarries.

When God asks us to wait for Him, He expects us to trust that He is coming and will not be late. He doesn't want us to go back into the world and give up on His return. He is on His way and will not be late, even if He doesn't arrive at the time we think He should.

PAULINE CREEDEN

~*~*~

Please continue reading for your bonus:

101 Faith Notes

WHAT IT MEANS TO BE A CHRISTIAN

1. One of the common misconceptions about Christians is that once you've been covered by Christ, you no longer sin or make bad decisions. But that's not true. The difference is that when we fall down into the pit of sin, we don't stay there. Christians get up and get going again.

~*~*~

2. For though the righteous man falls seven times, he rises again, but the wicked are brought down by calamity (Proverbs 24:16)

~*~*~

3. No matter how far away from the Master we have wondered away, He will search for us and call us until His work is complete.

~*~*~

4. Being confident in this, that He who began a good work in you will carry it on to completion until the day of Christ Jesus. (Philippians 1:6)

~*~*~

5. You have to think differently, and agree with God that what you have been doing is sin. It does not matter whether you were willful in your sin or if you sinned "accidently" – the response to the

knowledge of the sin must be the same: repent.

~*~*~

6. The Ninevites believed God. They declared a fast, and all of them, from the greatest to the least put on sackcloth. (Jonah 3:5)

~*~*~

7. The first step in repentance is to agree with God that you have sinned and stop reasoning with yourself that you are okay; that what you're doing is not sin.

~*~*~

8. If we confess our sins, He is faithful and just and will forgive us our sins and purify us from all unrighteousness. (1 John 1:9)

~*~*~

9. Yet to all who did receive Him, to those who believed in His name, He gave the right to become children of God. (John 1:12)

~*~*~

10. Unfortunately sin has this addictive quality to it. Once you start, it becomes so hard to quit. This is why God tries to teach us what we should avoid, calling it sin, so that we never have to learn to quit.

~*~*~

11. Through Him everyone who believes is set

free from every sin, a justification you were not able to obtain under the law of Moses. (Acts 13:39)

~*~*~

12. Jesus looked at them and said, "With man this is impossible, but with God all things are possible." (Matthew 19:26)

~*~*~

13. Is your problem bigger than the Earth, or more impossible to break than the creation of it? If God is powerful enough to create the heavens and the earth, isn't He powerful enough to help you overcome your sin?

~*~*~

14. Ah Sovereign LORD, You have made the heavens and the earth by Your great power and outstretched arm. Nothing is too hard for You. (Jeremiah 32:17)

~*~*~

15. I pray that the eyes of your heart may be enlightened in order that you may know the hope to which He has called you, the riches of His glorious inheritance in His holy people, and His incomparably great power for us who believe. That power is the same as the mighty strength he exerted when He raised Christ from

the dead and seated Him at His right hand in the heavenly realms (Ephesians 1:18-20)

~*~*~

16. A person born to Christian parents is not a Christian - he is a heathen. Although he would like to claim a heritage, a heritage will not give him heaven.

~*~*~

17. You believe that there is one God. Good! Even the demons believe that—and shudder. (James 2:19)

~*~*~

18. Anyone can say that he believes Jesus came to earth and died on a cross, he can even believe that Jesus was resurrected - but these are only historical facts and they cannot save him. And they do not make him a true Christian.

~*~*~

19. If you declare with your mouth, "Jesus is Lord," and believe in your heart that God raised him from the dead, you will be saved. For it is with your heart that you believe and are justified, and it is with your mouth that you profess your faith and are saved. (Romans 10:9-10)

20. If you have to see before you believe, than you can't call that faith. Faith is given before the miraculous event takes place, every single time.

~*~*~

21. Now faith is confidence in what we hope for and assurance about what we do not see. (Hebrews 11:1)

~*~*~

22. Then Jesus told him, "Because you have seen me, you have believed; blessed are those who have not seen and yet have believed." (John 20:29)

~*~*~

23. Who is it that overcomes the world? Only the one who believes that Jesus is the Son of God. (1 John 5:5)

~*~*~

24. Believing is seeing. The act of believing is an interior motive. It is what causes something to be true or false at least in our own minds.

~*~*~

25. For we live by faith, not by sight. (2 Corinthians 5:7)

26. Though you have not seen him, you love him; and even though you do not see him now, you believe in him and are filled with an inexpressible and glorious joy. (1 Peter 1:8)

~*~*~

27. God is not some distant, far-away, absentee father. No, He is present, He cares, and He doesn't want you to worry.

~*~*~

28. "Do not let your hearts be troubled. You believe in God ; believe also in me. (John 14:1)

~*~*~

29. Adversity and loss can often become the rudder by which our life is steered to come closer to God. We re-prioritize and discover what really has importance, and what remains shallow and unworthy of our time and energies.

~*~*~

30. That is why I am suffering as I am. Yet this is no cause for shame, because I know whom I have believed, and am convinced that he is able to guard what I have entrusted to him until that day. (2 Timothy 1:12)

~*~*~

31. We cannot be separated from God's Love, from

Heaven, from His salvation, from being His child and heir. Not even LIFE. Life cannot separate us from it anymore than death can.

~*~*~

32. For I am convinced that neither death nor life, neither angels nor demons, neither the present nor the future, nor any powers, neither height nor depth, nor anything else in all creation, will be able to separate us from the love of God that is in Christ Jesus our Lord.(Romans 8:38-39)

~*~*~

33. Notice that your hairs are numbered. I don't know about you, but every day I shed hairs. This means that God cares enough to know how many hairs are on my head today, because the number is different than yesterday!

~*~*~

34. And even the very hairs of your head are all numbered. (Matthew 10:30)

~*~*~

35. Almost every sin has its root in idolatry. We are busy trying to replace God: heal ourselves, make ourselves feel better, comfort ourselves, or solve our own problems. We become divided in our attempt to serve ourselves and God. This is all

idolatry.

~*~*~

36. Teach me your way, LORD, that I may rely on your faithfulness; give me an undivided heart, that I may fear your name. But you, Lord, are a compassionate and gracious God, slow to anger, abounding in love and faithfulness. (Psalm 86:11)

~*~*~

37. For by the grace given me I say to every one of you: Do not think of yourself more highly than you ought, but rather think of yourself with sober judgment, in accordance with the faith God has distributed to each of you. (Romans 12:3)

~*~*~

38. The Proud man can take care of himself. He's got things under control. He can find the solutions to all his problems. He doesn't need anyone's help.

~*~*~

39. Trust in the Lord with all your heart and lean not on your own understanding. (Proverbs 3:5)

~*~*~

40. The Humble man lets God lead. He understands

that he is not God and God is the one in control. He realizes that he cannot solve his own problems but looks to God for help.

~*~*~

41. I know, O LORD, that a man's life is not his own; it is not for man to direct his steps. (Jeremiah 10:23)

~*~*~

42. I run in the path of your commands, for you have set my heart free. (Psalm 119:32)

~*~*~

43. Enter through the narrow gate. For wide is the gate and broad is the road that leads to destruction, and many enter through it. (Matthew 7:13)

~*~*~

44. It's better to ask and receive the answer 'No,' then to assume the answer is going to be 'No,' and never ask.

~*~*~

45. But when you ask, you must believe and not doubt, because the one who doubts is like a wave of the sea, blown and tossed by the wind. (James 1:6)

46. Immediately the boy's father exclaimed, "I do believe; help me overcome my unbelief!" (Mark 9:24)

~*~*~

47. Therefore I tell you, whatever you ask for in prayer, believe that you have received it, and it will be yours. (Mark 11:24)

~*~*~

48. We are not strong enough to solve all our own problems much less everyone else's.

~*~*~

49. Jesus answered, "If I want him to remain until I return, what is that to you? You must follow me." (John 21:22)

~*~*~

50. You hypocrite, first take the plank out of your own eye, and then you will see clearly to remove the speck from your brother's eye. (Matthew 7:5)

~*~*~

51. You believe in me when I give up on myself, but will I believe in You when I am full of myself?

~*~*~

52. Keep falsehood and lies far from me; give me neither poverty nor riches, but give me only

my daily bread. Otherwise, I may have too
much and disown you and say "Who is the
LORD?" Or I may become poor and steal, and
so dishonor the name of my God. (Psalm 30:8-9)

~*~*~

53. You love me when I feel that I am un-loveable,
but will I love you when I don't FEEL you're there?

~*~*~

**54. What if some were unfaithful? Will their
unfaithfulness nullify God's faithfulness?
(Romans 3:3)**

~*~*~

**55. If we are faithless, He remains faithful, for
He cannot disown Himself. (2 Timothy 2:13)**

~*~*~

**56. Because you know that the testing of your
faith produces perseverance. (James 1:3)**

~*~*~

57. Today God has taught me that I don't
fellowship with the Lord because He needs it, but
because I do.

~*~*~

**58. Therefore let all the faithful pray to you
while you may be found; surely the rising of the
mighty waters will not reach them. (Psalm 32:6)**

~*~*~

59. Send me your light and your faithful care, let them lead me; let them bring me to your holy mountain, to the place where you dwell. (Psalm 43:3)

~*~*~

60. Be joyful in hope, patient in affliction, faithful in prayer. (Romans 12:12)

~*~*~

61. Oh Lord forgive me for not keeping my every thought captive to your obedience. How I pray Lord that I my progress and my witness will be seen by all.

~*~*~

62. Practice and cultivate and meditate upon these duties; throw yourself wholly into them as your ministry, so that your progress may be evident to everybody. (1 Timothy 4:5 NKJV)

~*~*~

63. We demolish arguments and every pretension that sets itself up against the knowledge of God, and we take captive every thought to make it obedient to Christ (2 Corinthians 10:5)

~*~*~

64. There are only so many hours in the day and we

only have so much energy. If we spend our resources on things that are unfruitful – that bring us down instead of raising us up, we won't have the resources necessary in order to help our fruitful branches bear more fruit.

65. I'm the true vine and my Father is the gardener. He cuts off every branch in me that bears no fruit, while every branch that does bear fruit he prunes so that it will be more fruitful. (John 15:1-2)

66. We need to put everything under the obedience of Christ. If it is not fruit bearing, prune it.

~*~*~

67. If your hand or your foot causes you to sin, cut it off and throw it away. It is better for you to enter life maimed or crippled than to have two hands or two feet and be thrown into eternal fire. (Matthew 18:8)

~*~*~

68. If I might occupy some remote corner of Heaven, the place farthest away from the Lord, but know that I have His approval - that would be huge gift.

69. Better is one day in your courts than a thousand elsewhere; I would rather be a doorkeeper in the house of my God than dwell in the tents of the wicked. (Psalm 84:10)

70. "Is God with us or what?" Don't we contend with God and ask Him if He's "with" us – on our side, doing what we want Him to do? Don't we constantly need proof that He's here for us instead of just trusting that He is?

71. And he called the place Massah and Meribah because the Israelites quarreled and because they tested the Lord saying, "Is He among us or not?"(Exodus 17:7)

72. God does not and should not fear us. We are to fear and to respect Him. Just because He loves us and takes care of us, doesn't mean that we lambs can tell the lion what to do. He could just as easily eat us as lie down with us.

73. Will the one who contends with the Almighty correct Him? Let him who accuses God answer Him! (Job 40:2)

74. If I am to take up my cross and follow Him, I need to count the inconvenience as nothing when it comes to bringing one person the love Jesus has for him.

~*~*~

75. Then Jesus said to them all: "If anyone would come after me, he must deny himself and take up his cross daily and follow me." (Luke 9:23)

~*~*~

76. You do not eat only once or twice per week. If you did, how much strength would you have? So don't think that going to church on Sunday or reading a chapter or two of the Bible per week is enough. Just like you have to eat every day, you have to eat God's word every day, too.

~*~*~

77. Jesus answered, "It is written: 'Man does not live on bread alone, but on every word that comes from the mouth of God.'" (Matthew 4:4)

~*~*~

78. But his delight is in the law of the LORD, and on his law he meditates day and night. (Psalm 1:2)

~*~*~

79. Do not let this Book of the Law depart from your mouth; meditate on it day and night, so

that you may be careful to do everything written in it. Then you will be prosperous and successful. (Joshua 1:8)

80. For you to have peace and tranquility in your life, you'll have to change your behavior outside of the prayer closet, as well. You cannot spend an hour of devotional time in the morning and evening and live like a heathen the rest of the day. This is no life change.

81. I have been crucified with Christ and I no longer live, but Christ lives in me. The life I now live in the body, I live by faith in the Son of God, who loved me and gave himself for me. (Galatians 2:20)

82. Wouldn't you love the freedom of knowing that you do not make mistakes? If you take every decision to God and He answers how each decision is to be made - you can be at peace and know that you didn't make a mistake, because all is in HIS hands.

83. Show me your ways, O LORD, teach me your paths. (Psalm 25:4)

~*~*~

84. Seven times a righteous man will fall, and seven times he'll get back up and keep going. (Proverbs 24:16). This has been extended to seventy times seven by Jesus in Matthew 18.

~*~*~

85. Then Peter came to Him and said, "Lord, how often shall my brother sin against me, and I forgive him? Up to seven times?" Jesus said to him, "I do not say to you, up to seven times, but up to seventy times seven." (Matthew 18:21-22 NKJV)

~*~*~

86. No matter how many times we fall, we've got to pick ourselves back up out of the pigpen and keep going. This is what we are called to do - to pick up our cross, and follow Jesus - for His burden is easy and His yoke is light - because HE carries it with us.

~*~*~

87. **For my Yoke is easy and my burden is light (Matthew 11:30)**

~*~*~

88. Let us always praise His name - in times of joy, in times of tribulation, in times of sorrow, in times of victory, and in times of defeat. When we feel the most depressed, the farthest from God - let us praise His name, even when we don't FEEL like it -

because the sounds of God's people praising God makes the powers of darkness tremble, and gives us victory even when we feel defeated.

~*~*~

89. For great is your love, higher than the heavens; your faithfulness reaches to the skies. (Psalm 108:4)

~*~*~

90. The Bible is full of ordinary people who went to impossible places and did wondrous things simply because they decided to obey God, even when others said "You can't do that."

~*~*~

91. The crowd rebuked them and told them to be quiet, but they shouted all the louder, "Lord, Son of David, have mercy on us!" (Matthew 20:31)

~*~*~

92. The doors God sets before us are much like grocery store entrances - the doors seem closed, but the minute you step up to them, they open.

~*~*~

93. You will not have to fight this battle. Take up your positions; stand firm and see the deliverance the LORD will give you, O Judah and Jerusalem. Do not be afraid; do not be discouraged. Go out to face them tomorrow, and

the Lord will be with you. (2 Chronicles 20:17)

~*~*~

94. God opens the door the minute we step up in faith. But if we never take the step of faith, the doors will always be closed.

~*~*~

95. Moses answered the people, "Do not be afraid. Stand firm and you will see the deliverance the LORD will bring you today. The Egyptians you see today you will never see again. The LORD will fight for you; you need only to be still." Then the LORD said to Moses, "Why are you crying out to me? Tell the Israelites to move on." (Exodus 14:13-15)

~*~*~

96. "A loser is a person who quits. Because if you believe in yourself, and keep trying, even if you fail over and over again, eventually you'll win – you're not a loser until you give up."

~*~*~

97. Let us not become weary in doing good, for at the proper time we will reap a harvest if we do not give up. (Galatians 6:9)

~*~*~

98. The temporary pain and misery of this time will be worth the results, worth the splendor, the dignity,

and the beauty. We must not give up. We have to remember that God has promised this threshing will not go on forever.

~*~*~

99. Does one crush bread grain? No, he does not thresh it continuously, but when he has driven his cartwheel and his horses over it, he scatters it [tossing it up to the wind] without having crushed it. (Isaiah 28:28 AMP)

~*~*~

100. The beauty of what is inside us will be revealed without being bruised, crushed, or destroyed.

~*~*~

101. A bruised reed He will not break, and a smoldering wick he will not snuff out. In faithfulness He will bring forth justice (Isaiah 42:3)

###

Please continue reading for the first portion of

The Prodigal Life

Introduction

Jesus Prayed: **"I have given them your word; and the world has hated them because they are not of the world, just as I am not of the world. I do not pray that You should take them out of the world, but that You should keep them from the evil one. They are not of the world, just as I am not of the world." John 17:14-16**

We are not of this world. It was so important that we know this, Jesus said it twice in this one prayer. Because we are not of this world, the world hates us. The world is miserable and because misery loves company, it wants us to be miserable, too.

Our life on this planet is so confusing, demanding, and hard. There are times when we feel so burdened that we wish we could just fly away to heaven already and be done with it all. We need to remember that God promised to never place a burden on us that we can't handle. If you're here on Earth, it's because God believes you can handle it.

So we have to wade through the muck of lies, ungodliness, and hatred. We have to be diligent and search for the truth. We have to keep our eyes on Jesus so that we can be kept from the evil one. The world has lots to say about what will make us healthy, happy, and whole. God gave us the choice to believe the world, or believe Him.

It all comes down to two choices. Over and over again in the Bible, God gives us this choice. Choose life or choose death. Choose the old gods or choose Him. Choose yourself or choose Him. Choose money or choose Him.

Sometimes we make the right decision. And sometimes we waver in that decision. Sometimes the answer doesn't seem so cut and dried. Sometimes it seems easier to curse or deny the God that "gave" us these problems than it is to praise Him.

So what do we do when we find that we have made the wrong decision? What do we do when we've fallen for the lies of the world?

God knew from the beginning that we would not be faithful one-hundred-percent of the time. He knew that the world would try to choke us like weeds. Jesus gave us the warnings, and told us what to expect. Even better, Jesus gave us the picture of what to do when we found ourselves neck deep in the world's muck and ears filled with the world's lies. He gave us His word, His truth, and He gave us the parable of "The Prodigal."

We've all heard it a million times. We know the story so well, that we probably only skim it or skip it all together when we chance upon it in our daily devotional. But we need to remember that ALL God's Word is for each of us. It is not this part for you and that part for Joe down the street. All of it is personal.

When we become children of God, He intends all the word to be ours. It tells us how to live so that we don't make bad decisions when the time comes. It tells us what to do when we've made a bad decision and need to make amends with God. It helps us to understand the deep, unconditional love which God has for us that we will not find in this world without Him.

When we understand that the whole word of God is meant for us, we might find new eyes to look at the life of "The Prodigal". We might even find that we are in one of the stages of his life. Take a look at those stages with me, and see if you don't find places where you can relate. I know that I can connect with each and every stage.

Many of us forget that the prodigal son was first and foremost a son. He was not a stranger who rebelled against God. What this means is that though we think of people who lived a rough life and then had a conversion later on as prodigals, that is not who this story is intended for. It's for sons. It's for God's children. It's for those of us who are Christians, who come to God and accept Him as our father. Then after accepting Him, some of us go astray. Some of us become prodigals, and go through these stages.

Understanding and connecting with each stage of the prodigal is important, because by doing so we can progress to the next level. In that progression, we will find growth and the Father waiting for us to come home and be His child. And His child is what He has called us to be.

This book is written for those of us who are already God's children and have gotten lost and made wrong decisions. It's written to help us to have a greater understanding of God's grace and how He loves us and wants us to come home. I pray that as you read this exposition, you come to a greater realization of your relationship with God. Maybe someone will even wake up to the wrong choice they're making and realize that they've wandered away unawares. Either way, it is my prayer that the Holy Spirit will use this book to grow closer to you.

STAGE ONE – A Son of God

A certain man had two sons. And the younger of them said to his father, "Father, give me the portion of goods that falls to me." So he divided to them his livelihood. Luke 15:11-12

If we consider the story of the prodigal as a story of each of our lives, in stage one we are defined as a "son." This means that we are saved by grace. Our name is written in the Book of Life. If you have asked Jesus to be your Savior, and His blood covers your sins. You are a Christian. You have an inheritance that God will fully give you upon asking. You belong to Him and you are His child.

But you still have free will. You are God's child – but you may not act like it. No one acts like God's child all the time, except Jesus. You make mistakes. You make bad choices. You have wrong thoughts, and judge situations based on your short-sightedness. You are human.

So often we decide to try to run our own lives without God's regulations. We say "thanks for the inheritance, can I have it now and go on with my life the way that I want?" We want our independence, but we want to be "saved," too.

Therefore I say to you, her sins, which are many, are forgiven, for she loved much. But to whom little is forgiven, the same loves little. Luke 7:47

When I was younger in the Lord, I used to think that I must love little, because I was forgiven little. But this is not the truth. Who decided that I was forgiven little? Who decided that the sin stains on my life were so small? I did. I made that short-sighted decision. Because I became a Christian at such a young age, I felt that my life was about as close to "sin-free" as it could get. So I passed judgment on my own life and decided that I wasn't so bad.

This made me like the younger son, ready to take my inheritance and go on with my life. This is a lie of the world that has permeated the church today. We cannot continue to go on with life, doing our own thing, making our own way, once we have been born again. You have DIED to doing things your own way. You can only LIVE again as you take up your cross, daily, and follow Jesus.

And I was not forgiven little.

For whoever shall keep the whole law and yet stumble on one point, he is guilty of all. James 2:10

I was guilty of all, and I was forgiven much. This is where so many Christians go wrong. It's how we see ourselves. We forget that we are guilty of murder, because we have hated someone. We forget that we are guilty of adultery, because we have looked lustfully at another. We judge ourselves as "not so bad" and forget how much we have really been forgiven. We forget how much that forgiveness cost.

That forgiveness cost someone His life. If He had not died the sinner's death, we would have had to do it. My sin was worthy of a death sentence, and instead Jesus took the sentence for me. But you've heard that a million times, haven't you? I had already heard it a hundred times when I was twelve-years-old and came to Christ. It was already old news and therefore easily forgotten.

"Familiarity breeds contempt."

When we see a stack of unpaid bills on the kitchen table, we often forget that they are there, because they are always in the same place. There could be something important in that stack that needs to be paid yesterday. Unless we are in the routine of paying our bills immediately upon getting a paycheck, we'll forget the importance of what's there simply because we see it in the same place every day.

When we forget the value of what Jesus has done for our sin, we find ourselves trying to do things our own way. After all, we've gotten this far and haven't sinned "much". We're doing "pretty good" by our own estimation, so why not just continue on as we are going?

Some people call this "easy" faith. It's where we say the sinner's prayer and get saved then continue living the way that we want to live. Where's the cross? Where's the cost that Jesus told us to count before coming with Him? Unless we are taught exactly what we're getting into by becoming God's son, we forget all of our responsibility, and only remember the inheritance.

When we're stuck on the inheritance and forget the responsibility, then we make the same choice that the younger son made with his father in the parable. That's when we say: "Thanks Jesus for the free ticket to heaven. I'll take that inheritance, and continue trying to do what I can to be good. See ya."

STAGE TWO – Prodigal living

And not many days after, the younger son gathered all together, journeyed to a far country, and there wasted his possessions with prodigal living. Luke 15:13

Some synonyms for the word prodigal: wasteful, reckless, extravagant, and uncontrolled.

When we behave like a prodigal, we waste the grace that God has given us. We proceed recklessly through our lives without caring about God's law. We are extravagant in our self-indulgence, usually spending as much as we can on our comfort in an effort to make ourselves happy. We are uncontrolled by God, and lose all self-control (which is a fruit of the spirit, by the way) because of it.

Remember, this is the picture of a SON of God. This is a Christian who has chosen independence over living as his Father's son. This is a Christian who has decided that his own judgment of right and wrong was good enough to live on his own. And I have been guilty of this, personally.

Ponder the path of your feet, and let all your ways be established. Do not turn to the right or to the left; remove your foot from evil. Proverbs 4:27-28

When we have independence, we get to choose which way we go. Imagine for a moment that you give a boy

50 dollars and set him loose in the toy store. You will see that child waver this way and that way. Maybe he'll get a bunch of Matchbox cars. Or maybe he'll get one toy gun. Or there's even the chance he'll get three action figures. Then again, he might get a video game.

This wavering back and forth, this indecision is described in the above Proverb as turning right or left. And that's what we do when we are independent. We swing one way, then we swing the other. We can't decide or make up our minds. We are wishy-washy. Independence becomes indecisiveness.

The problem here is that we don't know everything, so we don't know what would be the best choice for ourselves. The kid in the store doesn't know which toy he will get the most fun out of, the one that will last the longest, and the one that he'd be most happy with. So the child waivers in his lack of knowledge and his fear of the future – and so do we.

Independence is counterfeit freedom. We think if we can make all our own choices and do our own thing, we will be free. But the opposite is true. By trying to be independent, we are attempting to take God's place as the ruler of our lives. We can never succeed at creating happiness because we are the created, not the Creator.

All our attempts at trying to create happiness fail miserably. We end up becoming slaves of this world. When we are trying to create comfort, we spend more money. When we are trying to create satisfaction, we eat more. When we are trying to create joy, we get lost in pleasure seeking. Because we are not controlled by God, this leads to adultery, alcohol, drug abuse, or any other sort of superficial happiness the world promises.

Each of these things (over-spending, over-eating, adultery, alcohol, and drug abuse) promise happiness, comfort and joy. But instead they give us debt, an unhealthy heart, a broken heart, a weak liver, and an unstable mind. Worse yet, they give us shackles of addiction that keep us from being able to quit doing them and leave us stuck in their trap.

All of these provide us with "instant" satisfaction, but also "fleeting" satisfaction. What kind of satisfaction is that? It's the reason that the song by the Rolling Stones states: "I can't get no satisfaction." It's pleasure that lasts for a moment but has no lasting fulfillment.

As human beings, we desire fulfillment. Momentary pleasure promises fulfillment, but falls short every time. The alcoholic thinks that just a little more alcohol will make him happy, but instead it leaves him sick, broke and hung-over. The easy woman thinks that if she gives in to the man she thinks she loves, he will love her. Instead, he usually leaves her. The food addict eats more and more hoping that the satisfying first bite will be repeated each time, but the food gets blander as they fill up. The pot smoker goes on to harder drugs in an attempt to get back that first high.

We are in a constant search for what will satisfy us, but everything this world has to offer leaves us empty, broke, and broken. Still we will keep searching for that satisfaction – that fulfillment in these empty things – until we hit rock bottom

STAGE THREE – Reaping

But when he had spent all, there arose a severe famine in the land, and he began to be in want. Then he went and joined himself to a citizen of that country, and he sent him into his fields to feed swine. And he would gladly have filled his stomach with the pods that the swine ate, and no one gave him anything. Luke 15:14-16

All has to be spent before we reach bottom. Every penny we have, every waking moment we spend on our constant search for comfort, peace, and satisfaction has to be gone. We will chase that dream until we can no longer walk. We will overspend ourselves, overtax ourselves, and overexert ourselves as we work for our dreams of independence.

Satan is shrewd. He makes independence look like freedom, though it is really slavery. And he makes promises that he never keeps, but we fall for them anyway.

No matter how many times those new shoes fail to keep you happy, you buy another pair anyway. No matter how many times that chocolate cake fails to satisfy me, I eat it anyway. No matter how many times that shot of vodka fails to bring us out of sadness, we drink it anyway. No matter how many times that random sexual partner fails to make us feel loved, we sleep with them anyway.

We fall for it every time, hoping that this time it will

bring us the happiness that we crave. But when the money is gone, when the scale tips past 250 lbs, when you lose your family because of your alcohol or drug addiction, or when your heart is broken because of your adultery, you find yourself empty and at rock bottom.

Often we look to a "citizen of that country:" a person in this world who seems to have it together. This could be a counselor, a dietician, a close friend, or anyone who might help us get out of this mess. But whenever we turn to another person instead of God, this ends in failure. All humans are flawed, not one of us truly has it together without God.

The harvest is past, the summer is ended, and we are not saved! For the hurt of the daughter of my people I am hurt. I am mourning; Astonishment has taken hold of me. Is there no balm in Gilead, is there no physician there? Why then is there no recovery for the health of the daughter of my people? (Jeremiah 8:20-22)

God is our healer. He wants us to turn to Him, not to another. Even when we do what the citizen tells us to do, we'll still find ourselves empty-handed, empty-stomached, and in the pigpen. Unless we find a person that points us back to God and a closer relationship with Him, then this helpful "citizen" will only lead us further into the pit.

Remember, the younger son was not in the pig sty until after he went to a "citizen" for help. And much of the time, that's how it is. Things seem to get better for a little while following someone's advice, but eventually, you land in the pit.

It's like these drug commercials for depression. You see them advertised on TV. The drug claims to help you with your depression, but may also cause thoughts of suicide, insomnia, and physical health problems. You could end up worse off than you were before you started taking the drug. More than likely, you will.

Once you've debased yourself this far, even animals seem to have a life better off than yours. I believe the pigpen represents depression. It's when you are so low that you could not possibly get any lower. The pigpen is when you are dirty, tired, hungry, homeless, and helpless. It's the position where there is no worse place to be. You are dirt, scum, and it's hardly worth living anymore.

Thoughts of suicide might even come into your head. You definitely think to yourself that you would be better off if God would just take you now so you wouldn't have to struggle this way anymore. But God has you here in this place for a reason.

And we know that all things work together for good to those who love God, to those who are called according to His purpose. Romans 8:28

This is a miserable place, but it is for your GOOD. God is interested in breaking the strongholds Satan has in your life, and it's going to hurt a little bit. But God has promised that this testing, threshing, and dross removal won't go on forever, so hang in there!

This process feels so difficult, but the rewards are

incredible. How many of you have heard that a seed must "die" before it can grow? When I heard that story, I always heard about the seed's death, burial, and growth into new life. Most of the time, the concentration was on the burial and the new life, no one wants to talk about the seeds death.

The "death" of the seed comes when it is threshed. The outer covering of the seed needs removal. In order to keep the seed from being exposed to the weather and insects, the plant develops a covering over the seed. In order to make the seed right for planting, this covering must be removed. The removal of our own personal "covering" (the part of us that has become ugly and tough to protect us from the world), God must thresh us too.

Oh how miserable it is to be threshed!

Wait and think for a moment how miserable it is to be in labor, giving birth. Misery knows no bounds when it comes to travailing in childbirth. But the reward for the labor comes when the child is born. Suddenly the labor takes a backseat, forgotten, ready to be gone through again for another child.

That is what the threshing is all about. The temporary pain and misery will be worth the results, worth the splendor, the dignity, the august, the beauty. We must not give up. We have to remember that God has promised this threshing will not go on forever.

Does one crush bread grain? No, he does not thresh it continuously, but when he has driven his cartwheel and his horses over it, he scatters it [tossing it up to the wind] without having crushed it. (Isaiah 28:28 AMP)

Did you catch that? He doesn't thresh forever, and He scatters it before it is crushed. God has promised that the pain will be for a short time. The beauty of what is inside us will be revealed without being bruised, crushed, or destroyed. God has a plan. We only need to hang in there and trust Him.

STAGE FOUR – Realization and Repentance

But when he came to himself, he said, "How many of my father's hired servants have bread enough to spare, and I perish with hunger!" Luke 15:17

Finally, we remember who it is that really has it together. We remember that in our Father's house, people don't settle for pig slop, but have more than enough happiness and joy! In our Father's care there is happiness, joy, and yes, FREEDOM. We find all that we've been searching for on our own but have been failing to find.

Our minds begin to open to the fact that there is no better, happier place in the world than to be in our Father's care. We realize that His ways really were best all along. We come to find that the only thing the world has is an empty promise. Freedom is where we find happiness, joy, and our Father.

This means that we come to the place of repentance. What is repentance, and how do we do it?

Step One: Agree with God

When we sin against God, there are two ways that we can do it. One way is pure ignorance. We didn't know that it was sin, and so we honestly didn't mean to. The other way leads us down a road of denial –

we either "reason" and decide that it's not sin, or we lie to ourselves: God will forgive us, so we can go ahead and sin anyway.

God asks us for repentance as the only way to restore our relationship with Him. Repentance literally means to change your mind. You have to think differently, and agree with God that what you have been doing is sin. It does not matter whether you were willful in your sin or if you sinned "accidentally" – the response to the knowledge of sin is the same: repent.

If you deny that what you are doing is sin then you will have no reason to repent. You have nothing to "change your mind about." This is the person who thinks that he is just fine in the pigpen, and he has no reason to change his circumstances. So the first step to repentance is to agree with God that you have sinned and stop reasoning with yourself that you are okay; that what you're doing is not sin.

Step Two: Turn Away from Your Sin

Now you have to turn away from your sin. Easier said than done, right? Unfortunately sin has this addictive quality to it. Once you start, it becomes so hard to quit. This is why God tries to teach us what sins we should avoid so that we never have to then learn to quit. It really was for our own benefit in the first place.

In essence, this is when we pull ourselves up out of that pigpen and start on the road back to our Father's house. Again we have two choices. We can either stay where we are, or get moving. We can choose to turn to God or we can wallow in our pigpen and declare that the journey is too hard. It's when we decide if it's harder to walk home or harder to starve in the pigsty.

Step Three: Living a Life of Regret

There are many kinds of regret, and we have to choose which life of regret we are going to lead. Will we regret that we have sinned, and never do it again? Will we regret that we did not make peace with God and repent? Will we regret that we did not do enough for His kingdom by putting Him first in our lives and spending time with Him?

If we live the life of godly grief and regret the sin that we have done in the past, it will push us toward not doing it again. If we are truly sorrowful and feel remorse over the way that we have grieved God and destroyed our own lives, then we will loathe returning to the path of sin.

Do you think for a minute that the son wanted to return to the pigpen? Do you think he even gave it a second thought? I don't believe he considered returning once to the "citizen" and asking him to take him back once he started on the journey to his father.

In order to be in the same place as the prodigal son, we have to feel and understand the loss that we have experienced through our sin. Our sin robbed us of our joy. Just like any other idol, it made promises that it cannot keep. The overweight person doesn't feel better about themselves by eating more, they feel worse. The addicted person always has to have more and more of the alcohol or painkillers in order to feel the same kind of relief that they got the first time, and it was never a cure to begin with. The adulterer does not find true love in any of the relationships that they play in, and they are killing the love in the marriage that they have or could have.

By living a life of regret we guarantee that we will not return to the old one. If we remember the pain that the sin has caused us, we'll keep it at bay. By putting the sin in prison for robbing us, we can keep it from having the power to put us in its prison.

Step Four: Changing Your Behavior

It's time to give up. Give up on the sin and stop acting that way. Give up on trying to live your own life, your own way. Pull yourself up out of that pigpen and head home – and never look back.

This is what repentance is all about. Once you decide you want to change, you get up and start moving in God's direction. It's that simple. It's that hard. Luckily you don't need to do this entirely on your own, but God gives you the strength to overcome.

STAGE FIVE – Becoming a servant

I will arise and go to my father and will say to him, "Father, I have sinned against heaven and before you, and I am not worthy to be called your son. Make me like one of your hired servants." Luke 15:18-19

When we finally come to the awareness that we want our Father back, we often forget about His grace. We are stuck in the rut of independent living and think that we can earn our way back into our Father's house. We can serve Him, and if we do a good enough job, He'll let us back in.

This is where we try to battle our addictions before coming back to His house. We don't want to bring our food, alcohol, sex, and drug addictions with us to our Father's house, so we try to kick these habits all on our own. Because our motivation is pure, we might find success for a little while, but soon we slip back into the pigpen again.

We try and fail. Try and fail. Try again, and fail again. We think we're getting God's help to get us out of the rut because we are trying in the name of God. The reality is we are trying to pull ourselves up by our own strength. We are moving forward asking God to bless it instead of asking God and waiting until He tells us to move forward.

This kind of Christianity is similar to bulimia. You

starve yourself of your sin, and seem to be doing well, until you fall off the wagon. And like the bulimic, you binge big. You don't just sin little, you sin big. You stay in that pigpen and wallow in the mud a little bit. You fill up good on that sin.

Then the Holy Spirit gets a hold of you, and you purge. You repent just as big as you sinned. You cry and ask God to forgive you and help you do better. You claim the blood of Jesus, and start over again, trying to be perfect on your own. You take it seriously when Jesus ordered: **"be perfect, therefore, as your heavenly Father is perfect" (Matthew 5:48).**

When we try and try to overcome on our own, we only find one thing: We have slipped into the shoes of the servant instead of the sandals of the son.

The Bulimic Christian understands the grace of God to forgive his sin, but he doesn't understand the grace of God to OVERCOME his sin. Because this prodigal had never "sinned big" before he became a son, he's never had to overcome his sin before. This is a new experience for him. Because this same prodigal has been trying to be good on his own, he tries to overcome the sin on his own, too.

Failure is the result of the Bulimic Christian. Binging and Purging – Sinning and Repenting. Sooner or later this leads the Christian into one of two lives. Either he finds his way home, or he ends up like the "other son."

STAGE SIX – Coming Home

And he arose and came to his father. But when he was still a great way off, his father saw him and had compassion and ran and fell on his neck and kissed him. And the son said to him, "father I have sinned against heaven and in your sight, and am no longer worthy to be called your son."

But the father said to his servants, "Bring out the best robe and put it on him, and put a ring on his hand and sandals on his feet. And bring the fatted calf here and kill it, and let us eat and be merry; for this my son was dead and is alive again; he was lost and is found." And they began to be merry. Luke 15:20-24

When we repent, God runs to us. He loves us and refuses to allow us to be His servant. We are His child, and He would never have us be anything less. The pig mess of our past can be made clean if we let GOD clean it instead of trying to clean it up ourselves.

Lean on God. It's when we realize that we are weak and can't battle the addictions on our own that we allow God to battle for us. He will fight for us. Like a true Father, He wants to rescue us and do everything for us. He loves to spoil us.

When we finally find that we have been too weak to battle our sin on our own, we realize that God must fight the battle for us. By living in our sin and trying to battle the sin ourselves, we've been living in idolatry.

Almost every sin has its roots in idolatry. We are busy trying to replace God: heal ourselves, make ourselves feel better, comfort ourselves, or solve our own problems. This is all idolatry. If you are obese, chances are that food has become your idol – and you comfort yourself with it. If you are an alcoholic – you are trying to make yourself feel better with alcohol. If you are a drug addict, you may be trying to heal yourself by killing the pain in your life. And if you are an adulterer, you may be trying to find a way to solve your marriage problems by finding a new mate (before even breaking the covenant of marriage).

These sins that I have described are probably some of the most addictive of all sins. And it often seems so impossible to stop. Impossible to turn away from the food that smells and tastes so good when you feel bad about yourself. It seems too hard to stop drinking to drown the troubles of your day. It's equally impossible to suffer the pain when it's so easy just to take that painkiller. And falling into the arms of the person who you think loves you more than your spouse is too hard to give up.

Genesis 18:14 – Is anything too hard for the Lord?

Jeremiah 32:17 – Ah, Lord God! Behold, You have made the heavens and the earth by Your great power and outstretched arm. There is nothing too hard for You.

Matthew 19:26 – But Jesus looked at them and said, With men this is impossible, but all things are possible with God.

Is your problem bigger than the Earth, or more impossible to break than the creation of it? If God is powerful enough to create the heavens and the earth, isn't He powerful enough to help you to overcome your sin? The question is not whether or not God can do it, but rather how do we tap into His enormous power so that we can overcome this great obstacle which is in front of us called 'sin.'

Matthew 6:33 – But seek (aim at and strive after) first of all His kingdom and His righteousness (His way of doing and being right), and then all these things taken together will be given to you besides. AMP

Zephaniah 2:3 Seek the Lord {Inquire for Him, inquire of Him, and require Him as the foremost necessity of your life}, all you humble of the land who have acted in compliance with His revealed will and have kept His commandments; seek righteousness, seek humility {inquire for them, require them as vital}. AMP

The answer really is that simple: Seek the Lord. If you make Him the foremost necessity of your life (Spending more time with Him than anything else), by asking for Him (through prayer) and inquiring of Him (through the reading of the Bible), then you will be seeking the Lord and finding His power being given to you through the development of your faith.

It is only when we succumb to the fact that we are weak and powerless to resist our sins that we rely on God to do the impossible and teach us how. This is when we become the son rather than the servant. When we stop trying to be a servant and start acting like a son – we finally have the freedom to love Him back.

We become sons when we put God in charge and give up all our worries and our temptations. He will take control of them all and begin the good work that He's already promised you. He called you an overcomer, He called you victorious. It's time to become what God has already promised you that you are. It is impossible for God to lie. (Hebrews 6:18) So when He calls you MORE than an overcomer, He will make you into one.

Philippians 1:6 – And I am convinced and sure of this very thing, that He Who began a good work in you will continue until the day of Christ {right up to the time of His return}, developing {that good work} and perfecting and bringing it to full completion in you. (AMP)

He will not only begin this work in you, but He will complete it. Do not give up and turn back to your old ways. Don't get weary in following the right way. Renew your strength and draw closer to your Father through continual prayer, praise time, and reading of His word. (This is our personal trinity – discussed in the second half of this book.) All these things will teach you about Him and the more you learn, the more you'll love Him.

Through obedience and loving our Father we will bear the fruit of the spirit. If we abide in Him throughout our day, then we will be looking for ways to help His children. Drawing closer to God will cause you to abide in Him, making the impossible seem possible after all.

God has enough servants. They are called angels. When He created us, He wanted sons and daughters. If we come home to Him, and let Him love us as His children, we will find the freedom we desired all along.

.

STUCK IN STAGE FIVE – The Other Son

Now his older son was in the field. And as he came and drew near to the house, he heard music and dancing. So he called one of the servants and asked what these things meant.

And he said to him, "Your brother has come, and because he has received him safe and sound, your father has killed the fatted calf."

But he was angry and would not go in. Therefore his father came out and pleaded with him.

So he answered and said to his father, "Lo, these many years I have been serving you; I never transgressed your commandment at any time; and yet you never gave me a young goat, that I might make merry with my friends. But as soon as this son of yours came who has devoured your livelihood with harlots, you killed the fatted calf for him."

And he said unto him, "Son, you are always with me, and all that I have is yours. It is right that we should make merry and be glad, for your brother was dead and is alive again, and was lost and is found." Luke 15:25-32

Remember earlier when I talked about the Bulimic Christian? Now the older son here is an Anorexic Christian. He is so stuck on seeing himself as a servant that he shies away from all sin and condemns those that don't. He didn't really want a party for himself: he just wanted to have one offered to him so that he could turn it down.

Just as the Anorexic denies herself any pleasure in food, the Anorexic Christian denies himself any pleasure in Jesus. They are the "Christians" who have no joy. They are the ones who go around trying their best in doing all the work for the church that they can, but don't have a loving relationship with the Father.

This denial of joy in the Lord is shown in the Anorexic Christian's lack of love. If we look at the definition of love found in 1 Corinthians 13 and compare it to the actions of the second son, we will see how he falls short. I am using the Amplified version here, verses 4-7.

Love endures long and is patient and kind, love is never envious nor boils over with jealousy,

When the second son refused to go in to the party, do you think he was patiently waiting outside to talk to his father? Or was he boiling over with jealousy, impatiently waiting to have a word with his dad?

Love is not boastful or vainglorious, does not display itself haughtily. It is not conceited (arrogant and inflated with pride);

Was the second son boasting of his accomplishments and dutiful behavior or did was he humble? I think an inflated person is easy to make boil over. The second son displayed himself and his "obedience" as though no one had noticed. In his mind, no one had noticed enough.

(Love) is not rude (unmannerly) and does not act unbecomingly.

The disrespect this son is showing to his father is rude to begin with. Not to mention that it was a snub to refuse to go into the party and send the servant to fetch his father.

Love does not insist on its own rights or its own way, for it is not self-seeking; it is not touchy or fretful or resentful; it takes no account of the evil done to it (it pays no attention to a suffered wrong).

This son kept account of his behavior and his lack of reward for "these many years." He insisted on his own rights, and he was resentful for it.

(Love) does not rejoice at injustice and unrighteousness, but rejoices when right and truth prevail.

It seems to me that this brother was happy when his brother was in the pigpen. At least in the pigpen, "just desserts" prevailed. Likewise, the second brother did not rejoice in the forgiveness and mercy shown to him.

(Love) bears up under anything and everything that comes, is ever ready to believe the best of every person, its hopes are fadeless under all circumstances, and it endures everything (without weakening).

This brother did not believe the best of his prodigal brother. In fact nowhere in the parable did it say that the prodigal had anything to do with harlots, but this brother believed the worst and decided he did. He did not hope that his brother kept any of his father's teachings at heart. He did not know, but he assumed the worst.

In his serving of his father, this son kept account of everything that he did while he worked. He kept a tally of what his "payment" received entailed. He forgot love. He forgot mercy. He was so busy working for the kingdom, that he forgot his brother.

God doesn't want slaves and servants – He wants sons and daughters. He doesn't want us to be stuck on trying to be good. He wants us to **"Love the Lord your God with all your heart, with all your soul, with all your strength and with all your mind, and love your neighbor as yourself." (Luke 10:27)** By doing this, you are seeking the Kingdom of God. And by doing this, by seeking the Kingdom first, all the rest, all the self-control and perfection that you desire will be added to you.

This self-imposed slavery known as Anorexia may make you feel like a success, but you will be miserable. You will have no charity toward those who are not as "holy" as you because those who can't control themselves the way that you can are not worthy to be in the same place as you are. This makes it harder to love your neighbor as yourself.

Only by relying on Jesus' strength instead of your own can you find Joy in the Lord. Only then can you understand that the burden you bear is supposed to be shared with Him. Only by leaning on Jesus can you learn to love Him and love those who He places in your path.

No matter how well you think you are doing, consider: is the joy of the Lord what people see when they look at you? Do you honestly feel like you've been in the sinner's shoes when he finds forgiveness in Jesus? Or do you condemn his lack of obedience and don't understand why the Father would ever forgive and love him?

Check yourself, check your heart, and check your love. Being an Anorexic Christian is being inflexible. You are determining yourself, your rules, and your judgment to be above God's. Your neck is stiff and your eyesight is narrowed by your lack of nutrition. Feast with the Lord, understand that "all work and no play makes Jack a dull boy." God did not mean for you to work only.

For John came neither eating nor drinking, and they say "He has a demon." The Son of Man came eating and drinking, and they say, "Look, a glutton and a winebibber, a friend of tax collectors and sinners!" But wisdom is justified by her children. (Matthew 11:18-19)

So do not forget that Jesus did not go around Galilee with a stern expression and an anorexic, inflexible manner. No, He was eating and drinking, partying with tax collectors and sinners. So how do you feel about those sinners? Even when that sinner is your brother in Christ? Do you welcome him back and

145

join in the party with your Father? Or do you turn away with your stern expression and go back to serving?

Again I say, do not be a slave – be a son!

…Continued in

The Prodigal Life: Coming all the way home to God

Available at Amazon

in Paperback & Kindle Edition